ANCIENT LIGHTS

ISBN 978-0-9866909-6-9

Edited and designed by Elizabeth Adams
Cover illustration by Rosemarie O'Toole

First Edition

Published by Phoenicia Publishing, Montreal
www.phoeniciapublishing.com

Printed in the United States

ANCIENT LIGHTS

Selected Poems

Dick Jones

PHOENICIA PUBLISHING
MONTREAL

Table of Contents

To my kids, first and second editions,
and to Emma.

STILLE NACHT

On the night
that I was born,
the bells rang out
across the world.

In Coventry, in Dresden,
the cathedral bones sheltered
worshippers with candles,
witnessing the ruins.

In Auschwitz-Birkenau,
the story goes,
the death's-head guards
sang, *"Stille nacht,*

heilige nacht". Their voices
slid across the Polish snow.
The sweetest tenor was Ukrainian,
the man they called Peter the Silent.

He never spoke and he killed
with a lead-filled stick.
In the Union Factory, packing shells,
they dreamed of Moses.

In Horton Kirby, fields froze
and ice deadlocked the lanes.
My father rose in the cold
blue-before-dawn light

and cycled sideways,
wreathed in silver mist,
to the hospital. Each turn
of the track betrayed him

and scarred by thorns and gravel,
he bled by our bedside.
My mother laughed, she remembers,
as the nurse administered.

"Been in the wars?" she asked.
Outside, across the Weald,
from out of a cloudless dawn
the buzz bombs crumpled London.

Outside a town in the Ardennes
Private Taunitz hung
like a crippled kite
high in a tree.

A cruciform against the sky,
he seemed to run forever
through the branches,
running home for the new year.

Outside Budapest three men
diced for roubles
in the shelter of a tank.
Fitful rain, a moonless night.

Sasha struck a match
across the red star
on his helmet, the red star
that led them to this place.

Extra vodka, extra cigarettes,
a rabbit stewed,
the tolling of artillery
to celebrate the day.

The blackouts drawn,
December light invaded.
We awoke, slapped hard
by the early world.

Our siren voices
climbed into the morning,
a choir of outrage,
insect-thin but passionate.

Through tears our parents
smiled: within the song
of our despair they heard
a different tune.

And as our voices
sucked the air, swallowing
the grumble of the bombs,
only the bells survived.

ANCIENT LIGHTS

1. *1945: Emannuel Road*

Banded light, I should remember first,
from the bottle-green, ruby-red window.
Soused in colour, wordless,
I kick air, anticipating dance;
beat palmless hands together,
finding rhythm. From another room,
through formless darkness, shellac hisses
introducing flaring danceband brass:
Carrol Gibbons, Henry Hall.
My parents foxtrot through my light, in love.
I sing the blues.

Dad and Monty had a decent war,
home-guarding Clapham Common,
listening for the 'cello hum
of bombers, then the woodwind of incendiaries.
Crouching in the doorway
of the burned-out Coach and Horses,
they evaluate the midnight orchestras,
mark them out of ten, emerge,
pissed and applauding,
to the siren's lone soprano.

2. *1952: Norbiton Avenue*

The day they told us
that the king had died
the church bells at St John's
were inconsolable. The wireless news
came wrapped in Handel
and my mother, ironing in the kitchen
froze, the bright hoof hovering above
creased sheets. On the trolleybus
to school, passengers stared
at their hands. The conductor haunted
the stairs in black. We crooned,
adrift through empty streets.

3. 1952: Latchmere Road School

In the Assembly Hall shoes barked
across the blockboard floor as we jolted
into fishbone lines. A monstrous silence
bound us; we forgot to speak. My eyes
slid, panic-stricken, across scraped heads
and blazer backs to the black bands
on the teachers' folded arms, to the melting
ice-cream colours of the Union Jack,
loose-furled beneath the portrait of the king,
to the glaucous sea-green light
that pressed against high windows.
When the hymn broke like the first wave,
least expected, I was caught broadside:
brute music from the baby grand, slammed
hard; the ragged engine of four hundred voices
grinding against the tide. Seized
by a greater grief than my own (motiveless,
unfocussed – who was this king
who had died in bed, not by the sword
in battle?), I sobbed. What did I hear
unlocked inside those throats? What broke,
shook loose and rattled down the centuries
before my birth? That calling out to an old god,
so far from song, an ululation thickening
the air and silting up my breathing.
Gathered up into a lavender bosom,
I was hustled into daylight and a thin
persistent rain. Faceless, my guardian,
she rocked me, rocked me, the two of us
riding at anchor on a dim swell of voices,
storm-broken, soughing like an old wind.

4. *1954: New Sherwood*

What do you do when,
from dream to mortar,
you build a school?

Is it like building a house
with the values locked
into the discipline of bricks

on bricks? Or is it like
the building of a church,
into which somehow

you must incorporate
the numinous, the hushed,
the obedient? (Here

the story's easier to tell
behind rich windows, in
the organ's smoky voice.)

Or is it like a glass
solarium, *prima vera*
all the year, an investment

of light, the incubator's
catechism chanting hare's foot
weeping fig and fern

to glory; fruits exotic,
hand-reared and fat
and green and uniform.

Don't build. Just find intact
(albeit cracked and leaky)
a house that's there already,

one that's rooted
firm and knows its skin;
that's free of pain

and ghosts, with trees
and half-forgotten gardens,
mossy cold-frames, twisted

vines and sudden sundials
in the long, uncultivated
grass. Then let us blow

like puffball parachutes
in a random wind,
the achene fruit

that falls and germinates
at random when
and where it will.

MR MOORE'S WALL-CLOCK

Mr Moore lived in a lean-to shack
(two-roomed and shingle-boarded) at the back
of the barn where Grandad kept his car.
Clad with roofing felt and thick with tar

which bubbled in the sun, it shrunk
into the lee of the outbuildings, sunk
deep in a reef of marigolds and nettles,
like the old shipwreck that tilts and settles,

shapeless and unnoticed now. In the long days,
we children wound our orbit round pathways
of cinders, followed the beaten circuits through
bluebells and cabbage-patches, flew

back to the cottages like swifts at sunset.
And the world was one green hill, the sky a net
that trawled us through the seasons. Time
was a circle dance, two hands in rhyme,

turning, trapped, around the Roman face
of Mr Moore's Prince Albert watch. And time and place
conspired: early summer, watch chain swinging
in the sun; a crowd of heads inclined to hear the singing

of the wheels. Snapping the brass lid shut,
he muttered, "Tempus fuggit", and withdrew. Cut
free from the web, we reeled away
around the orchard tracks. And then, one day,

one June, I crouched inside his smoker's bow
beside an empty grate. Outside the undertow
of low clouds hissed against the single pane,
rattling nettles, damping dust, a trailing rain

from the east. Granny plumped his pillows, twitched
the patchwork counterpane his wife had stitched
in the days of the old queen. Now he lay
log-still, dream-bound and seventy years away

along the parabola of Vinson's paddock, chasing
painted ladies with his cap. Granny fussed, replacing
flowers unnoticed (borrage, oxe-eye daisy), winding up
the lamp-wick, slipping the sill of a china cup

beneath his Kaiser Bill moustache. And I lay coiled
in the cage of the hearthside chair, breathing oiled
darkness, ghost fumes of black tobacco,
calcium tang of lime and plaster, a scent-echo

of caves, primeval places. And behind the chanting
of the rain, a tenor voice called time, counting
down the seconds: Mr Moore's old hanging clock, walking
across the wall on one brass leg, soft-talking,

like the messenger whose tale is too important
to be shouted loud. Not this harbinger's way, to rant
about decay, the end of worlds. So, doomed,
I watched and heard the hours unwind, consumed

by the oldest story. Mr Moore slept and there I dreamed
for the last time. And how brief the story seemed -
the fable of the wheel that turns from light
into shadow, from my midday to Mr Moore's midnight.

FIRST ECLIPSE

A full eclipse, they told us:
bit by bit, a feeble daytime moon
will efface the sun, enfold us
in a counterfeit of night at noon.

Around the edges of the lunar disc
a crown of fire will burn so bright
that scrutiny by naked eye would risk
blindness. Thrilled, we learned that light

that violent must be sifted
through a darkened lens. And so
the grownups stood about, eyes lifted,
penitents in sunglasses who know

the world's about to end. Meanwhile,
we children lay in long grass, sharing
out the negatives I'd brought – a pile
of family snaps from home. Pairing

them up like playing cards, I dealt,
choosing for myself a glossy square
of clouds on a bright black day, and knelt
(like a penitent) to outstare

the slow mutating sun. Indistinct
at first, but then, from partial darkness,
bold and clear, Mum and Dad, arms linked,
strode out of their past. The starkness

of that moment's image – of their smug duality
before my birth – was blinding and I dropped
my hand. Lost in eclipse, I couldn't see
where light began or where the darkness stopped.

SHEEP ON THE BROWN HILL

There are sheep,
hopeless, round-shouldered clouds
of wool. They have the eyes
of demons

yet the mouths
they clamp round nettles
seem innocent of teeth.
They have the cloven hoof

yet their legs
seem afterthoughts, a child's
charcoal lines
drawn at all four corners.

Knee-high again,
I hang like a casualty
on the barbed-wire fence,
gaping, contemplating

sheep in orbit
around the hilltop house.
No route or destination;
no sense of purpose

to be found within
this witless shifting traffic.
I look for patterns,
signs of navigation.

Sun moves through thin clouds;
wind wraps the house,
sings in wires.
Sheep crop and shuffle

all day long. Nothing alters
on the brown hill.
One generation inhales;
its descendants sigh.

I am an old coat now,
stretched on thorns.
Night slides across and finds me,
purposeless yet blessed.

NIGHT POACHERS

Full moon
bold as a cry,
clean as new ice.

Two men running
noiseless across
frozen fields.

Gin traps in
canvas bags
rattle like teeth.

They fall laughing
in clouds into
the lee of a wall.

A dog barks;
a man calls.
The sounds curl away.

The men sleep
wrapped around
their prey
like lovers.

PHOTOS

What makes light, wakes us;
what shapes light guides us inside days.
We drink it through our skin; we are
wet with its silver scales. It sticks
through holes like big nails, scratches
us and we bleed light back. It squirts
out of sudden conduits – broken windows,
shifted curtains, open doors, It drips
from leaves, cleaning them greener,
slides like mercury released; it flows
up slopes and hides behind shadows.

Light must spill over all we are
and all we do. Light alone survives us;
We die in open places and light
will shine our bones the whiter.

Note: *photos* is the Greek word for "light."

WATER

The original form
of flesh, it moves,
animate, but boneless.

Consider vapour. Steam
in the breath
of cattle, from the

dawn grass. Water sprinting
millionfold for the
limitless deserts

of the air. Water
drunk. Water falling
in its soft lattices

over our bodies.
Water with skin.
We sink beneath

its flat top,
flesh on flesh,
beneath its stiff

meniscus. Such mating
with the pellucid self
of water joins the circle

of our time here.
Unboned, we assume
the property of dream.

SHOOTING AT A FOX

Up on Bell's Hill, hours
after sundown; watchless
thus timeless; starlight printed
on the earth below:

all the lights of Exeter
in a black bowl. We breathe
through our mouths. No wind
in the hillside beeches

or the hawthorn hedge
we crouch behind. Bob looms
at my side, log-still,
indistinct, yet electric

with attention, his cradled shotgun
staring at the ground,
round-eyed. An owl quavers
in the ice-heart of the wood.

Movement at the field's edge: shadow
on shadow; an elision of shape
and formlessness. The fox slides
along a dark rail, single-

purposed, the fanatic's way -
hand over hand through
the long grass
at the field's edge.

Bob's gun coughs twice,
dry-voiced. Night cracks
like slate; splinters fly
and the world tips up.

We stare, bloodshot, jangling,
into the bright darkness.
Shadows realign at the field's edge.
Night self-heals, like water.

NIGHT COMES IN

Late evening.
I step outside.
At first the dark
means nothing

but conclusion.
Then the pocked
light of a few stars
and a sliver of moon,

creamy but tart, like
apple sliced, and
through trees
a fragrance of bells.

HITCH WOOD

Hitch Wood. Beeches crowding the gloom,
green mansions and their galleries,
mezzanine terraces under a million tiles
each one laced against light and the steep rain.
Above, invisible jets stitch up tomorrow's skies.

ROS RUA

1. On Cashel Hill

"And you tell me that he vanished,
out on the hillside. Nothing found,
no body, not a trace of where he'd been
or where he'd gone?"

She topped the Guinness, placed it
like a sacrament upon the bar.
We studied it. "Oh no", she whispered.
"Disappeared completely. But…"

(she grinned and moved away),
"they've seen him late at night
still looking for his sheep, O'Faherty.
Just a shadow by the burial ground,

whistling up his flock". They laughed
and tipped their pints. I laughed
and raised mine too. Through the door
of Boulger's Bar the day was

Connemara silver-grey. Peat fires burning
in July – the tint of them
on the edge of a salt breeze
in from Cashel Bay.

Later, high up Cashel Hill
the fog came down like wet wool.
Blinded, I perched on rock,
only my breathing shifting

the warp and weft of it. Close-knit
into that fleece of wraiths and phantoms,
robbed of a milky distance of bays
and mountains, I could speculate

the ghost of O'Faherty, white
on white, footsure, eternal, stepping
across the tussocks like a dancer.
I rose and followed him down,

a twisting fume inside smoke,
and stepped back into watery sunlight
amongst the gravestones
in the burial ground.

2. *Looking for U2*

And word came down from Boulger's Bar:
Bono, The Edge, those shades, that stetson hat,
two bags of groceries from the minimart
next door, an Audi TT kicking gravel into
Cashel Bay and heading down the mile
of rocky track towards Ros Rua.
For me behind binoculars, stretched along
the dry stone wall, the music clinched it.

Wired to the sky like summer smoke,
a melody ascended, needle thin, undefined,
above the low-pitched mossy roof into
the afternoon. (I saw them wedged in primitive
splendour: Bono, the Edge on a broken sofa;
Mullen, Clayton, heads together, tracks
mixed onto minidisk, a picture window
open to the pale sun, the breathing sea).

Stalked by gulls, mobbed by gorse, I crawled
like a lone commando down where the fields
broke cover over rocks, down where the swallows
stitched the sky to water. Voices crooned
in the telephone wires, a heartbeat away
from the green front door. (Bono, The Edge,
a bottle of Mouton Cadet blanc between them;
Mullen trailing a pensive finger round the rim
of a crystal glass, Clayton watching
the bobbing seals in Bertraghboy Bay).

And then the door swung wide
and the music bloomed like a tin flower:
Daniel O' Donnell singing *The Rose of Tralee*.
And a four-square farmer's wife came stepping
high over the tussocks, scarved and booted,
ringing a bucket like a broken bell.

And she's singing too, singing in a wild
soprano, keen as the edge of a spinning
slate, plaiting her voice around O'Donnell's
skinny tenor, scattering the gulls and lifting
a fishing heron out of the shallows
and into the all-accommodating sky.

BALEZINO STATION

At Balezino Station we disembark in silence
under the great arch of night. First
whispers leave breath hanging, shining

like bright smoke. The old moon
leans through cloud. A silver wind
blows the stars about like spray.

A tide of trees floods the half-dark,
sucks at the line's edge. Motionless,
we diminish, here at the junction between

two hemispheres. Behind us bloodless territories
of turned soil and domestic waters
and beyond the taiga, the first forest

to come tumbling out of the young dreaming
of the world. And now the thin edge
of an eastern wind brings tears of resin,

a scent of green disorder, a cataract
of leaves and berries far ahead. Darkness
crowds us back onto the train. Rocked

but sleepless, we sit and stand by night-
curtained windows, watching the dim images
of ourselves watching the flying trees.

BIRDS ON THE CHUSOVAYA RIVER

High flat sun, sour light
draining like whey
through muslin cloud.
This bird's geometry – square-winged,
turning on the axis
of its hunger, reorders
the sky. The berkut, summer eagle,
sideslips into the treeline.

Where the river croons
over stones, where we drink
from clear channels, this bird
scars the water's skin. The swallow,
stippled in the ribbed water, turns
on a wide wheel centred
in a blue orbit.

Night's sheet is torn
at the corner. This bird
has a knife in its voice.
It slides on a wire,
the owl, from maple
to beech, a yellow light
in its eye and acid
on its tongue.

Night rain boils in the river.
Young moon hooks clouds
into ribbons and rags. This bird,
the heron, rising from the reeds,
climbs on its long arms
from dark towards light.

GRASSCUTTERS IN SVERDLOVSK, 1990

Across that single wide flat road, potholed
all the way to Moscow, we were told,
grasscutters move like dreamers through a gauze
of dust. An old man stoops and slowly draws

the dry stalks into shocks. Then next, a child
hefts with a pitchfork twice his size the piled
grass onto a cart. Between the shafts
a cartoon horse shimmies its tail through drafts

of summer flies. Behind, at the other side
of waste ground, lifted on a crooked tide
of flats and billboards, Uncle Lenin gazes
po-faced from the recent past, appraises

the shifting grass, the painted sky behind
and a red sun sinking fast. Wall-eyed, he's blind
to the eternal – this, the steady, slow
caress of a young man's scythe, the scavenger crow

dogging the mowers as the new wind twists and turns
the poppies' scarlet faces. Lenin burns
brief in the sunset. Then the shadows blur
that too familiar gaze and now confer

upon the flats the anonymity
of dusk. Rocked home in a crosstown tram, we,
the gilded pilgrims from the rotten West,
witnessed the ancient world – a horse at rest,

the stacking of the sheaves through dust, the drift
of a mower's scythe, the steady lap and lift
of sleep, of reverie. A harvest, it seems:
a gathering in of those early summer dreams.

LEAD MINE, SWALEDALE

This hole is a clean wound
in the hill's skull. Turf
whiskers the rim, bedding

stitchwort and herb robert.
Wordless, I hang over
the broken wall, staring

into the bleak null
that is deep space
trapped. You lean out

like a gargoyle, poised,
gripping a stone.
Suddenly you shift

like a sleeper woken.
The stone slips from
your grip, turns once,

pedalling the air, then
drops dead straight
down the shaft.

We share the steep rush,
falling with the stone,
sucking air until silence

catches up our breathing.
Only the broad voice
of the moorland wind

at our backs, talking
with the gorse.
And then, from the gullet

of the earth, at the edge
of hearing, a chuckle,
deep and rich, coital,

celebrating congress, stone
on stone in a secret place.
Echo into stillness.

Changed and wordless, we scatter
down the hill, tuft
to tuft, heading for home.

CERTAINTY

Post-coitum, he relaxes back
into rumpled sheets, cat-happy.

His lover lies curled in sleep,
her back, her shoulders a trove

of moon-silver, her hair a coil
of gold. He watches through

the porthole - a city skyline;
cranes and barges slide away astern.

Her breathing rhymes with
the blood-beat of deep engines.

Land dissolves and light decays.
He sleeps, sea-dreaming miracles

and the ferry bears them forward
in a straight green line. Only over water,

such flawless symmetry: this
the brief geometry of certainty.

LINES

Straight talking,
that was what
was needed, so
you said. And

you smiled a thin
and final line,
and you turned,
as they say,

on your heel,
on a sixpence,
and you strode,
straight-limbed, along

the coastal path,
direct, unswerving,
to the jetty, walked
its slick rectangle

to where the ferry
tugged its moorings.
Just in time:
the straining lines

released, the cables
stowed, the ferry
drove a silver
track, straight as

a rail, towards
a flat horizon. And,
as I watched
unmoving, you

slipped at last
around the slow
unyielding curve
of the world.

GIRL WALKING ACROSS A FIELD

A girl is walking across a field, trailing
the sun on a long rope of light. She's eating
beech nuts, dropping the spiky velvet shells
like Hansel, to mark the journey home.

When she returns at dusk, it will be
the moon that tugs her stumbling over
the same tussocks, through white clover
where the beech nut shells still lie.

The sun is a fool for lovers, gold-hearted
and broad armed. But at the day's turn and
at the story's end, it's the moon that pulls
her long black tide over the world.

PETAL IN A BOOK

This is
a bloodspot,
a communion wafer,
a thumbnail manuscript.

It's a membrane,
a ghost of crimson,
a gauze against
white light.

It lifts
even now under
my down-breath,
lifts like

an insect's wing.
It was late summer.
The picking
of petals

was idly done.
No loves-me,
loves-me-not.
You laid them,

two of them,
on my eyes
like dead man's
pennies. I crossed

my arms. The sun
diminished. You
laughed and
fell back beside me

into the perfumed
grass. We murmured
and kissed. Larks
were singing.

Someone called.
We scrambled up.
One petal
sideslipped, scooping air.

The other,
a satin coin,
I placed between
two pages for

Raskolnikov to spend.
Forty summers later
the currency
is undischarged.

LUNATICS

We stopped the car beside
a nighttime field of barley, wheat
or root-crops. (Darkness dusted
all at ground level into grey).

Inconsequential anyway, beneath
a bold unclouded moon, full-faced
and staring us down, fresh
from the seat of light. Its power:

to generate and then regenerate,
to pull new tides, administer madness.
Oh, we wished the same but into
separate wells, deep and distant:

Deliver me safe and settle me
into the world – tomorrow,
tomorrow. Silent, we drove on,
chartless and compass-free.

BECOMING GHOSTS

There is a bucket of lights on the clifftop
squatting at the track's end and there is
the great swarm of the summer dark.
Its night-roots are tugged by the sea: its
black branches clog the pathway. We two
climb blind, naked still under towelling robes,
rime in hair and on lashes, love tattooed
in wheals of sand, communion salt on our tongues.
I smile into the darkness. Ahead of me, a thick
shadow, I sense you smiling too.

We're drawn by obligation and now, this late,
by shame a little: company is waiting on us –
above the shifting of the waves, voices rise
and scatter like sparks, music pulses. Soon –
another stumble upwards, one more turn
through gorse, its candles winking – we'll be of
the world again, restored, reconstituted.
From hereon, bleached by light, we'll turn into
a pair of ghosts, doomed, blessed to haunt
each other through the long years to come.

BETWEEN STATIONS

Between stations lies
what I call, *faute
de mieux,* the real world.

Long jawbones of houses,
each exposed like molars,
upturned and particular.

Here, a garden tricycle,
tilted onto a bony shoulder.
Fallen or pushed? And there,

beanrows and water features,
gouts of flowers, spilled
butter and blood.

And someone sleeping,
pinned to a blanket
like a specimen whilst

a girl in green
at an open window
waves a 'phone, yelling,

frozen, voiceless, a hanging
gargoyle. All so clear
then immolated at

a track's turning. This
is how our lives
walk and talk, coughing

syllables heard by no one,
throwing shapes that
are black against obsidian.

ROOM

"Up the wooden hill to Bedfordshire",
was your direction. And each night
I spent with you I would consider
that velvet gradient and breath

would catch and falter. So steep,
the climb away from firelight into
the half-dark shadowfields above.
Yellow bulbs that melted buttery hollows

into the hard darkness, the ghost-
scent of lavender, the bulk of a double bed,
a grounded barge, and the cold that hung
shimmering like the northern lights.

The cottage is gone now under the roads
that tie another world together. Cars
carry their interiors, brash, impersonal,
through different nightscapes.

Lights bloom within them like
clever flowers; sunless heat like
a birthright; motion as an imperative
in a land that would be still.

THE TIES THAT BIND

The morning after you left I drew
the curtains on the seven acre field.

Two hares were bowling through the stubble,
wind-blown, skidding like broken wheels.

They danced and sprung apart and danced again
and then were gone, beyond the tidemark

of the tree line. A mob of seagulls
swung downwind from the west, scattered,

gathered again in a brawl of wings and then
were gone, into a bleak neutrality

of towering clouds. Love or combat, the wind
blew them into the world and out again,

these dancers, bound only to the end
of their measures and not beyond.

STAIRS

Seen from this corner
of an empty hall,
the stairs. The wall at
an angle makes of them

a sharp, downward-pointing
triangle. The risers dwindle
from their full width
to a squeezed wedge, which

diminishes to nothing. And
yet somehow we can throw
the front door wide and
hit them running, home

from so far away. Or
we can scrape a leavetaking
through that nothing, heading
for so far away.

THE GREEN MAN

Trees are so certain, implacable,
even when fallen, each one
a manifesto proposing stillness

around a slow heart. Philosophers
out of the earth, they breathe
into the secret sky.

Where they reach with ease
and grace and find, I reach
to the sinew's length then dream.

To be straight and unencumbered,
carrying the shifting cargo high,
neither offering nor withholding;

to lodge song and let it go;
to save in green and spend in gold;
to dance a frieze against the skyline;

to observe impassive like Hydra
from a thousand faces, each one
bearded, lidded, rimmed in leaves.

THE SUN HOTEL, DEDHAM, 1954

I wake to the hysteria
of bells - medieval laughter
out of my stained glass dream.

Paddling Daddy's slippers
across bare boards (as black
and ancient as the mud

that silts up the Stour), I reach
the leaded window. Beyond,
the church squats on its bones,

brooding music. Hymns are hatched
stillborn; organ voices rage in vain,
quelled by the crowing of the bells.

The street in both directions
is innocent of cars. Phantom mist -
an atavistic veil - blurs outlines:

passers-by are cloaked and cowled,
pacing the tracks and byways
of their ancestors. My child's breath

smokes the glass. Morning thickens;
even the light seems ancient now.
Yawning, I curl back into

a tumulus of sheets. The bells cascade,
mocking the shape of my few years.
I sleep again and now, in the

mapless dark, my green heart
beats faster. Mine is the steady pulse
that animates this room; its beams

draw new sap from my source.
Plaster, lath and tiles expand; the house
tests its roots. The bells rejoice

a continuity of mornings. This,
the moment and the lost years,
are swallowed in their shining.

SUPERSTITIONS

Across my godless sky
a magpie skids,
a barcode flash,
trailing misfortune.

I paint a cross
onto the air.
And then that night
it's the full moon

bagged in clouds
swollen with snow.
I must drop
three wishes into

her milk-heart
before the clouds
hustle her away.
In a last heartbeat

of light, I invest
a trio of dreams.
But silently, as if
to confound negotiation,

snow fills the bowl
of the universe,
the sky falls to meet
the rising earth

and the seams
are drawn. White
darkness, a breast
of feathers. Without

my lodestars, compass
spinning, this sailor
must dead-reckon
his course alone.

BINNERS

Superstructure

Even then it was a dour anachronism, beached
at the tideline of a bleak estate, a great beleaguered
pile - Victorian hubris raised in red brick precipices,
gothic crenellations, totem chimneys, tottering over

fields of scalloped slates. Built by honest burghers
to house the footsliders, the wobblers, the pagan
visionaries, the nihilists, the fallen doves. And the pile
squatted on its hill of bones, hoarding in reality

a sad communion of cockeyed optimists, lost souls
whose only act of madness was to let loose hormones
in their teens like red balloons, old crocks and crones
beyond repair and one or two of the truly damned or blessed.

Infrastructure

I work in the asylum laundry,
dawn 'til two, forking bedsheets,
wet and grey like tripes,
into the drums to cook.

Booted and wrapped, shiny
white in oilskin aprons, angel
butchers, we move through steam,
feeding the ironing room.

We, the furtive and the cruel,
duck behind nicknames, aiming
to pass unnoticed or unchecked
within this strange nation:

Fish, the foreman, with the
glaucous eyes; me, the Monk,
for my pelmet fringe; and
crew-cut Stig of the lipless

v-shaped smile, like a deft
two-stroke razor slice. Ours
is a realm of clouds, high windows
sweating kitchen dew and vaporous

doorways like dream portals, blurred
against white streaming tiles. And
passing between these shape-
shifting airlocks, the strange

quotidian traffic. We sidestep
their world like unshelled crabs,
sidling our tasks between sheet
heap and drum, heads down

and purposeful, breathing only
our own air. And they move
between us in their own
fashion: the dancers, shapeless,

ageless in their smocks,
spinning and turning to
secret tunes in undiscovered
keys; the counting man

who circuits the vast estate,
enumerating fetishes – certain
lintels, keystones, door handles,
a smoked glass windowpane,

a beech tree root, tapping
each one with crooked
magic forefinger and then
moving on to realign

some other crucial fuse
while the sun is high.
(I watch him secretly,
like a bobbing bird at work);

and last, within the dust
of the parade, precarious
as a shard of glass,
Red Mary. Fizzing on

the threshold, she tests
the air. Her top lip
puckers, lifts over
a black bucket of

horse teeth. She snickers
and pushes at her brush-
fire hair, a corolla
of torn flames, the colour

of rust. Pale, pale
blue eyes switching and
slipping, making of the world
a place of fumes

and snapped filaments, just
an inkblot atlas to guide her
through black land
and fathomless sea.

And it's here and now,
within the splay and straddle
of her limbs inside the doorway,
between one clumsy

heartbeat and the next,
that there might be
deliverance – a rough facsimile
of love as nurse or porter

turns her round, the pressure,
gentle, solicitous, the voice
a fuzzy burr, back along
white corridors, white corridors.

But no one's there
and Stig is sprung-wound
and ticking close beside me.
I can smell his musk

through boiled linen and suds.
Dipping armpit deep into the drum,
he tugs out cotton knickers,
red as a haemorrhage,

and dangling the deep, sad
weight of them like a toreador,
he edges forward. His thin rudiment
of mouth beaks into a pouting kiss

as he sashays onto the walkway
where she stands. In that sweat-
heat, she is, in this moment,
rabbit to his serpent.

Fish draws hard on a cigarette
and turns away, but I am
complicit, witness from the start,
hiding amongst the rank

garment foliage like a naturalist,
sensing that what must now
transpire will strip us
to the quick. Clocks stop

inside that doldrum pause.
And she begins to keen,
a sound thin and high,
like wire hard drawn

through the membrane of
the air. And Stig two-steps
sideways, flicking the bloomers,
chanting on a breath:

"Crazy Mary, crazy bitch,
come on and fuck me, crazy
bitch, come on", and laughing
high and wild like a child

on a rope over water,
innocent and dangerous
in the free air. He dances,
now scampering forward

and back, forward and back
under a blood-red flag.
The air shimmers and stiffens;
then Mary shatters it like

a huge pane of glass.
There is a quality
of sound – the mud-born
eructation from the throat

of a marsh bird, or
some searing midnight
heartbreak called from ridge
or hillside – that curls

around the edge of time
to bear witness to what
we have never known,
should never have to know.

And Mary shrieks from that
elemental place, her mouth
split earth and her voice
magma, sudden and naked

in the wrong world. Stig
stops dead, poised like
a mural dancer. This
raw noise has clogged

the air into something
like fog or dynamite
and our ears ring with it
and we can't see for tears.

Stationary, rooted, like
a screaming tree, she flails,
ululating from within the
perfect storm, an ecstasy

of rage, crystal-pure and
targetless, uncorrupted by
concern or issue, red-raw
but of itself, primordial.

From this spotless light,
this impeccable heat, stars
and their matter draw
their source. This is

the ultimate release,
a hideous, intoxicating
freedom. Like some twisted
Breughel sower, she scatters

the molecules of reason
into this coruscating wind
and for its duration
both of us are blasted white,

Stig and I, reamed as clear
and vacant as blown eggs.
And now inside the cone
of silence that crowns

the thunderclap, we stand,
Stig and I, each in
his moment, the one
a still life in white and red,

caught at the edge
of the breath before
panic animates; the other
a dumbstruck initiate,

hearing in the soaring
engine of the scream
a wild music, seeing within
the beating Shiva arms

a terrible beauty, the purity
of free-falling water, the
rootless, boundless liberty of
the infant and the lunatic.

Is this how we sunder
gravity, leave the earth
and fly? Is this shame
I feel or yearning?

They come for her and,
with unconsidered skill, they
truss her as she stands
and bundle her away.

The sounds diminish, dwarfed
and dopplered through the
labyrinth beyond and,
in the laundry, drums

grind and roll and steam
embraces. But I am marked
now, an initiate. I know
of their mission this much:

that it's not to care
and cure but to contain
and then conceal. These
seismic forces must be bound

tight in Promethean chains.
Neither love nor freedom
can survive the fire from
what we might become.

I fork bedsheets, wet and grey
like tripes, into the drums
to cook. And I must wear
this secret like a scar.

INSOMNIA

Night. From the carbon window
I stare back, a deconstructed mask
amongst trace elements of moonlight,

rain, black leaves. I am part shapes
remembered and part shapes
from out of the sleep of reason.

In this shaft of silence just
before the dawn, the shadow
world is palpable: gods

and monsters glide and crawl
by my garden gate. Half-dreams,
uncertain memories blow like feathers.

Here and now, I sense,
is the sticking place where
all things meet: skeletons into flesh,

ghosts into plasma, rumours, fears,
the whole arcana hard wired
into the dark. No sound this side

of the distant rhyme of a long train
running. The night and I, strange
company in a world without hours.

And then, when I turn away,
there's just my breath
and the falling rain.

TESCO: THE FRUIT AND VEG

I'm lost amongst the fruit and veg.
Smacked onto a sandbar of bananas,
I draw breath. Time enough to plan

a cross-stream paddle to where
tomatoes roll. Confusion now:
do I choose from the mighty crowd

of bobbing heads – *hoi polloi* love apples,
teeming and jumbled like a marathon?
Or should I deal directly with the nabobs:

big red bandits, glossy warlords riding
four to a boat, privileged, a bounty on
their heads? I buy down-market

then plunge hands wrist-deep into
new potatoes. Green and brown
and honest with dirt in their ears,

they swarm into the bag, snub-nosed
and stumpy, laughing like it's
Friday night and opening time.

Then suddenly I fetch up on exotic shores.
I am a sallow stranger, a grey alien
in this territory of paw-paws, giant

pineapples, lichees and mangos, prickly pears.
Even the grapes glow silver at the core
like eggs from Mercury. Translators help us

with instructions: *Peel the skin*
and then remove the stone. Good
in salads or with demerara sugar.

Not for me: theirs is a harsh tongue.
Even colonised like this, flushed from
their jungle fastnesses, they lie

implacable in their alien beds.
My fruit bowl's crafted for the humble
apple, orchard pear, domestic plum.

I tip the guards and cross the border
back into a land of rain and wind
and kitchen sink and garden gate.

STAINED GLASS

The quality of light: this, a piece
of late evening sky. How darkness
can shine: last of the sun, a first
breath of stars, a waxing moon.

Judas walks out of the small room
while they are still dining.
No one knows but Jesus
and his head is turned away.

But they can't escape, these
protagonists, caught between
the ruby and green, the dark blue light,
the black bands of lead.

WAVELENGTHS

#1. iMac 2.66GHz Intel Core 2 Duo

I paddle the keys and pixels break surface
like bubbles. The blue window shivers into a spray
of letters, uniform, a lingua franca. The world and his wife
are talking hard, a promiscuity of speech that melts
into the pool, unvoiced. This is language out of light,
words squeezed and shredded out of shape and form,
electronic runes and glyphs squirted into bits
and bytes down filaments. These digits, these encryptions,
they're mouthless, lost in space. No tongues or lips
articulate the cries and whispers of the slave electrons
working the binary roads. Behind the brilliant lexicon,
just the insect voices and the hum of spinning disks.

#2. Icom 756 Pro Mk II HF transceiver

Still dark outside. 05.00 zulu and a cold wind
rocks the antenna tower. I'm beaming west
on 20 meters, listening through the chuckle
of morse, the whooping heterodyne. I'm looking
for Australia on the long path, vaulting scraps
of landscape and the great bare, muscled back
of ocean; skidding in across the eastern shores,
magnet-voiced and listening hard. A VK3,
a loner by two hundred miles of fence-line;
a little wooden house, a splinter in the prairie skin.
Just him, his wife and daughters, fixing the broken wire
that separates the cowboys and the kangaroos
from dreamtime. Now the aerial image shimmers,
breaks. I lose his voice as the skywave shifts,
lose his tale of full moons, crowding stars
and voices in the wind. I drift with the tidal ebb
and flow of distant storms, spikes of wireless sound

and silence. But I've spoken; he has spoken.
Breath has shaped and joined our words.
We have thrown a line across the earth
and tugged it once or twice.

LOVING

Love has always been for me
something of a thicket. Turning
in my own breadth has backed me
into thorns even as I've reached

for blooms. Trapped, I guess, for
the duration, like the deer hunted
through brakes and bowers then
found motionless, terrified, waiting.

SEA OF STARS

They will require,
should I return,
that I give name
to all the things I saw.

Even as I feed back
voltage, trickle chemistry
past their electrodes;
even as I share

my heartbeat with their monitors,
my blood with their microscopes,
they will question
in quiet voices,

seeking out new nouns
with which to corner
the ineffable, new verbs
to charge the immaterial.

As now their aerial voices -
filtered through ionosphere,
the shingle-clouds of asteroids,
across these tideless oceans -

whisper insubstantial, needle-thin,
scratching their need to know
the unknowable onto the mighty
silence. I trail interrogation

like a shower of sparks.
But from this eminence
I no longer heed
their eyes that scrutinize,

lidless, unswerving. This dark
accomodates a billion eyes,speculating
my parabola by day, by night, probing
for my tiny skidding light.

Implacable, incurious, I navigate
the brilliant wastes - long black
sargassos drifting, planet wrack
and flotsam, dereliction.

And beyond, always beyond,
the bright flying splinters of the stars.

LOSING MY RELIGION

Implacable, yesterday's twin magpies,
throwing shapes across my path.
Impervious, the button moon tonight
sitting in my toplight, casting its cold

favours into some other upturned
face, over the hills and far away.
My religion: counting down
the telegraph poles against a dream,

a wish, a promise. Make it right, make
it right or here and now I'll turn my back
on this captive fire and walk across those
starless fields where no light shines

and no paths wind towards the unnamed
horizon. Let the compass spin and
the lodestone crack; I'll take my chances,
blind, tideless and alone.

AN HOUR IN CHAPEL ANNEXE

What are we to believe? That Christ
welcomed the thorns, Sebastian the arrows,
Catherine the wheel? Yes, they tell us.
Only when the body's shriven, mortified,

made carcass and dispatched
can the soul emerge immaculate
and rise like gas, invisible yet palpable.
Pain is the passport to Jerusalem.

Christ hangs on above my head, his face
cast down, his arms stripped wings
spread wide, his ankles crossed. This
is more dance than agony, a frozen

entrechat – Christ terpsichore, reeling
down the ages to a timeless tune,
treading out the double loop, the bee's
infinity, until the measure's known by all.

And what's a dance? A means by which
we occupy the air, divert, persuade,
seduce. Passionate engagement, yet
powerless to lift the curse of Sisyphus,

or block the juggernaut, or move the stone.
This God omnipotent, who claims our praise
and swallows our prayers like a hungry bird,
is from dreamtime. He draws on the oxygen

of our need. We might well worship
water falling, metamorphic clouds,
the janus faces watching from the cliffs
that tell us what we want to know.

CREDO

I believe at the root
in breath as a first
principle. Breath –

the intake, the giving
out - is our signature
onto the air.

Next I believe
in the business
of seeing and hearing,

the processes of light
and sound whereby
we inhabit the cracks

and corners of the earth –
the guarded scrutiny
of strangers, the ear

cocked in a waiting room.
Incidental revelations,
accidental wisdoms.

As for mortality,
the cricket ticking
in the long grass

is timepiece enough
for me. Wound up
by the sun,

his spring uncoils
at night and
he dreams in black.

But, as a final article
of faith, I believe in
the heartbeat certainty

of two adjacent hands
on the parapet of
a bridge somewhere

touching, finger to finger,
and breath quickening
to mingle, and this

causing the sun to rise
and the moon to wax
and all the tides to run.

FLIGHTPATHS

1. *1913: Man with Wings*

The strangest of times: a skein of geese
crossing the bedroom window, heading west
and no body of water within seven miles.
I am playing the pagan - sleeping late amongst
the Sunday morning bells.
Heaven is a cloudless sky
in late September, harvest past,
leaves on the turn.

At first I think I hear the binder,
wheels beating, turning at the headrow,
but the fields are bare.
Such a beating, a clattering.
More geese searching for a lake
in this land of furrows? Or
the rector in his Wolsely
come to seek me out?

And then my window darkens
into the shape of wings, jagged wings –
Weston mill uprooted, reeling across the fields?
Certainly a hurricane of sorts
in the throat of this beast
squatting low over the beeches,
dabbling its feet in leaves, roaring
in a black updraft of rooks.

An aeroplane, fearful in the untried air –
nothing like the rising bird
it mocks, This is a man,
dressed in wire and canvas,
climbing out of the clover.
This is a godless man ascending,
out of the dust, towards the light.

2. *1940: A Dream of Aeroplanes*

A fire next time, I read. And when it came
it was sky-borne. Some had said at first
that out of it might come a cleansing;
out of the sky might fall a fire

bright and holy, prophecy fulfilled. September,
and I trimmed the ivy round the lych-gate.
It was lifting tiles clear of the joists
and my gardener was still in France.

That was about as close as the war
had come – censored letters, rumours,
like an invisible tide you can hear at the edge
of the world. Little to see beyond uniforms,

gas masks in boxes, gummed paper stretched
over windows. And then, that afternoon, flying west
and in and out of cloud, the planes, a geometry
of crosses. I watched and all around

the earth stood still. The organ voice
of their passing scattered rooks, rippled
the water in the rain-butt, rattled a latch.
And then we carried on, conscious only of a sniff

of autumn in the air, the planes forgotten
in an empty sky. That evening we were told
of the bombing – docks ablaze, the tram wires down,
parish halls as hospitals. But still it came

from the wireless voices, morning papers and
the travellers' tales at the village bar. Birds trilled;
I picked a sprig of yarrow for my hat, and rain
rushed across the lead roof of the transept.

The Messerschmidt came. Not quite, as they say
in comics 'out of the sun': it was a dismal morning
stacked with cumulus. But we can all remember
from our kitchens, hayricks, lonely bedrooms

(I was in the vestry hanging surplices) the sound –
a falling cadence, like a voice that begins
in the throat but can't find words. 'Despair',
it would have said. We heard it, all of us.

But no one saw the plane come down,
just the gout of fire that coiled and spun above
the oasthouse. Then, when they searched
the fields around, those Home Guard amateurs

(the lads who filled my pews at evensong),
they found a booted leg, bloodless, like a spare part
brought along in case of need. Little Sammy Scase
took the joystick home and his granddad scraped

the handle clean. ('Viscera', the vet said later
in the milking parlour). Then it rained again
and the army came to haul away the wreckage.
And no-one paid for Vincent's oasthouse.

3. *1996: Flypast at Old Warden*

Even now, here, this past
before my past leaks down
the long conduits, the time-
channels, weed-locked with

my own memories. Back then,
on corner bombsite, in the
air-raid shelter under the apple trees,
that past before our past

bellied up, breathed in our faces.
Churchill, Hitler, Uncle Joe bowled
down cinema aisles and into
our infant dreams. Parents' stories,

shed headlines from old newspapers
feeding the living-room fire, comics
swapped in playground corners, Belsen
photoes, shifted sideways through

a conspiracy of desks - war-echoes
blew like late rumours from a world
still turning out of darkness. Our legacy
was smoke from fires still burning.

And now, trailing tails of smoke,
red, white and blue, the parachutists turn
and turn in a blank sky. The last Lancaster,
Spitfire, Hurricane tug their trinity

of shadows over the aerodrome, over
the lifted faces of the crowd, across
the eyes of old saluting men,
remembering. Their past before

my past speaks in the beating
engines, the ghost-passage of three
black crosses over September fields,
heading east to the world's edge.

SIMON WIESENTHAL LEAVES MAUTHAUSEN

Simon Wiesenthal leaves Mauthausen.
Is it spring or autumn? Birds are singing,
lining the wire in the long dawn rain.
Wiesenthal carries the bag the GIs gave him.

Smoking, they lounge in groups by their jeeps.
Maidens of war, they see all, know nothing.
Scorched earth, still warm. Maybe the victors
fired the villages, or the vanquished in retreat.

Ah, the villages, where they knew nothing,
where they toiled with their heads down
in the black wind. Now they group like cattle
lost amongst their cottages, their hayricks burning.

Wiesenthal walks in a straight line, one foot
placed with calculated care before the other.
Something like rejoicing trips his heart
as he approaches, step by step, a horizon

owned by no one. He won't look back.
The wire will bind his dreams until death
and towers will stand four-square at the corners
of every field and garden and voices will crack sleep

in countless rooms, strange and familiar.
Israel will be raised on a raft of bones. "It will
survive me. Now I must walk in a straight line
for as long as shadows fall".

AUGUST 6th 1945

Went shopping that day. In the square
flowers in bloom, but on the turn.
I noticed how there is a sort of grandeur

in the passing of flowers. Youth, the full flush,
cannot have it all. The trees were turning too –
a curl and twist to each leaf,

some falling, some fallen. Early, I thought,
too soon, too little time in the world.
I paused, put down my bags.

There is a bench near the post office.
I sit there in the summer, in autumn
and watch the birds, the children.

I sat there on that day and, leaning back,
looked up through the branches. Did I
see the 'plane or only hear it?

Three breaths, nine heartbeats. First the light.
And then the heat. And then the sound.
And only my shadow left behind.

DIE MAUER IST RUNTER

The wall is down. Incredulous
we contemplate, through raw gateways,
dawn in the West. You, the baker,
me, the busdriver, there the student
carrying a flag, there the woman
who cannot forget or forgive;
we move through rubble,
through the searchlights,
through the watercannon's crazy rain.

This is the real dance;
we stitch its paces
over the Kaiser's cobbles,
in between the Weimar tramlines,
through Hitler's broken archways, empty squares,
up and down the grim lattices
of Russian tanktracks.
Laughing, we invade the territory
inside each other's arms.

BIRTHQUAKE

He is hypothesis,
an act of faith, a theory.
He's rumour without
a name. What's the evidence?
Radar graffiti – a splash of
chalk dust in the dark.
"Look, you can see his hand!"
No, it's just a phantom
caught on polaroid, foam
blown off water,
cuckoospit, thistledown.

And yet we watch,
the two of us, solemnly,
breathing through our mouths,
seismologists on stakeout, waiting
for the independent pulse.
And there, and there again:
a ripple in the skin, miniature
tectonics; something stirring
at the core. He is on his way
from a dark place to break
the surface of the world.

IDIOGLOSSIA

Out of silence you release
a cataract of syllables:
consonants collide
and vowels burst
like bubbles. It's
a mash of nouns,
a dribble trail
of verbs. It's
three coins rattling
in a glass; a rippled
plait of water over
stones; beads falling
from a broken thread.
It's information, or
a disembodied song,
or verse unchained
from its syllables.
It's messages from
before your own blood –
time of the shared heart,
the underwater breath.

MAISIE SLEEPING

Your soft clock
scatters seconds like
peas on a drum.

A feather pulse
stutters in your
neck. Your bird-

breath barely lifts
the cotton strand
across your lips.

But, as I turn
away, a breeze
that has yet

to blow touches
your cheek and
you smile, lopsided,

arch, and life
rehearses in your
unaccommodated face

A BRIDGE OF DREAMS

Sitting here between you in the dark,
breathing hard from the stairs, your cry
my summons, I wonder where these boat

beds are floating you all tonight. I wonder
what kind of cataract spilled you and then
splashed you back. Is there for us a commonwealth

of dreams? I ask into the dark. Are you all
heir to my dusty fears? You lie across your beds,
beached starfish, the ragged pulse of nightmare

flickering behind your eyes. I try to read
its narrative through shadow and across
the years. Is there, then, a great pontoon

of dreams, bound together like Xerxes' ships
across the bay? And may I cross it, boat
by boat and so go back, go forward?

REUBEN IN THE LONG GRASS

Easy to forget (and we forget
to our loss) blackberries at knee-
height. Like obsidian lanterns
carried high amongst spears;

or the glaucous light of gooseberries
shining like sightless eyes
casting the sky; or red angel
apples dancing in green clouds.

All these glorious impedimenta
to one hobbled and tripped by
couch grass and tussocks.

We must remember where
the world lives, we who occupy
the empty empires of the sky.

ROSIE'S DANDELION

Rosie brings in the last
dandelion, carrying it closed
in a chalice of hands like

a sacrament. Stock still,
she passes a slow thumb
around its bright corolla.

It lifts its head. We are charged
with its accommodation.
It lolls loud, a solo voice

in a wine glass. By morning
its royalty is spent. The crown
is sweated hair, the stem a bled

vein. Rosie cups its scrap length,
lifting it to me on a tear
for aid or explanation.

But what can I tell her
about time that I would
have her know so soon?

BAD LIGHT STOPPED PLAY

Alan said
(and Keith agreed)
it's when you get past sixty
that mortality's
an issue.
Wrists and fingers,
one time nifty,
crab and stiffen.
Easy catches miss you;
now, once-demon bowlers
slump in deckchairs
sipping whisky.

Keith remarked
(and Alan nodded)
that, like smirking boys, you're shifty
with the pretty girls.
They'll kiss you
on acquaintance,
but those misty
distant smiles are
painted onto tissue.
Fifty-odd and rising,
the scoreboard climbs
to tickle sixty.

EVENT HORIZON

I saw Eternity the other night
Like a great ring of pure and endless light...
Henry Vaughan

A dark treat, this doorway brush with death.
Expecting the shadow-flicker in his neck,
the guttering fuse, she saw that he lay still
and that fine silver dust hung in the air.

Silence boomed in her blood. She forgot
to breathe. She stared into the hole in time
through which he'd slipped. She saw dark wings
that beat too fast for angels', saw

the broken place where bones come from
and where bones return. All this in a heartbeat.
Wiser than scripture, swifter than light:
a destination on the other side of grief.

NIGHT RAIN

I sleep with the quarterlight
half open, tipped
like a questing lip
into the dark.

Night rain is falling
and the talk is all
of transformation: black
on black in threads

and swatches, gravity diamonds
heading south down window
panes; the air itself
partitioned into beads

and space. Fluctuation, shift –
this parcel of earth self-
ministers, self-heals. And I
bear witness whilst below

my body ticks backwards
like a novelty clock –
new times, new intervals,
deep secret bells and

slipping gears. Yes,
just outside, a skin
and filament away,
the heft of falling rain

in space, against
the leaves and on
the running earth
is like breathing.

MAL

Strange word, 'stroke' - a gentle sleep
and then you wake up,
changed. Caressed by infirmity
on the brown hill, kissed
by disability as you climb
the long drive. The farmhouse tips
and, heart in crescendo,
you embrace the grass.

Indifferent sheep manoeuvre,
crowding out your sky.
You lie in a lump, adrift
at the field's edge, floating
on the dead raft
of your limbs.
The sun nails light
into your one good eye.

Near dusk her scarecrow voice
scatters your crowding dreams:
she calls you from the house,
the sound of your name
curling out of the past,
a gull-cry, fierce, impatient,
tearing at the membrane
that has dimmed your world.

Root-still, potato-eyed,
you are another species now.
Your medium is clay and saturation.
Mummified, like the bog-man
trapped by time, you lie dumbfounded,
mud-bound and uncomprehending
as the sun slips down
behind the hill.

The urgent fingers
scavenging for a heartbeat,
fluttering like bird-wings
at your throat,
are busy in the dark.
You feel nothing
of their loving panic,
their distress.

All love, all optimism, pain,
all memory, desire coarsen,
thicken into vegetable silence.
A dim siren wobbles in the dark.
And then rough hands manhandle
your clod-heavy bulk.
Night swallows the spinning light
and closes in like smoke.

STILL LIFE

Each morning they organise your bones
into the wheelchair, stack you leaning
out of kilter. Thus I find you, wall-eyed,

feather pulse and mouth ajar. This is
a stillness you are learning as silence
silts up your blood. I name you: 'Mum',

I call, quietly at first, as if this were
only sleep and you might resent the passage
interrupted. But your shade is walking

a broken road on the far side of dreams.
I keep my coat on, lean in the doorway,
breathing in the alkalines and salts

that are your presence in this world.
Beyond, through narrow windows, rain
drifts like smoke. The trees shift

their high shoulders, hefting their leaves
like heroes. I can see the lift and fall
of their evergreen breath, the slow,

dispassionate pulse. Such senseless beauty,
propping up the sky as if there were no
tides turning or falling stars, no ashes to dust,

no time at all. You speak – a half-word,
cracked in the middle. Syllables drift
like fumes. Somewhere in that steam

of meaning, the filaments of memory:
the horn's tip of a lover's moon,
a song's dust, the eye's tail catching,

not quite catching, doorway phantoms,
window ghosts. Grief crosses my mind:
its hydrogen release – from local pain

to lachrymae rerum, all in one ball
of fire. Easy, it would be to cauterise
this lassitude, here against the lintel,

watching not the rise and fall of your
fish-breath, your insect pulse, but
the immortal trees beyond. Too easy;

but death looked in and turned away,
indifferent, and now it's down to me,
the blood-bearer, to wish away your life

for you. The house ticks and hums.
A voice calls out, thin and querulous;
another coughs. I turn down your light.

There, against the window, dusk outside,
you are becoming your shadow
cast against the shifting of the trees.

CLEAR BLUE SKY

My dad was a man of prose – a specialist: words used
like gardening tools to conjure shapes, to fashion patterns.
Language mattered: correspondence ran to pages –
letters to the council; 'thank you' cards to nurses
that read like testimonials. Even notes to the milkman
came across like billets doux to an old and valued friend.
And the writing: tiny box-shaped words in biro,
whispering in lines, or gathered quietly in the margins,
small-voiced but insistent, looking for truths.

When he knew that he was dying, he sat at the edge
of his life, scribbling a commentary. Twinges
from a cancer hotspot got a note immediately,
draped around the Guardian crossword clues
or squeezed between the calculations in his ledger:
where it hurt, for what duration, and, in imagistic detail,
the character of pain (like a voice, like broken glass, an ache
like winter rheumatism). And, towards the end, in his little diary,
potted phrases: "Slept well", "Insomnia", "Coughing still".

For we who sat around his bed, it was the silence
that confounded. To the nurses plumping pillows, lifting cups
from which he didn't want to drink; to waiting family
fiddling with the radio, sifting through his laundry,
he said nothing. All his words were spent just days ahead
of the breath that carried them. And then, the afternoon
of the day he died, the clouds drew back, late spring appeared.
Mum leaned back towards the window, smiled and said:
"Look - a clear blue sky", and we turned to see.

My father didn't turn his head. Whatever sky he saw
was far behind in time, or maybe just ahead. Whatever sky it was,
no messianic veil, no chariots of fire obscured the view.
His great abundance, just like ours, was absolutely empty –
birdless, sunless, silent and ineffable, mocking the mad commotion
down below. He drew in breath, breathed out and said:

'A clear blue sky', floating the words on the sterile air
like leaves. He didn't speak again; he died that night and,
one by one, the stars went out, a lexicon set free.

BEBEE ELLEN'S MERRIPEN

Sometimes they stand in twos
and threes at the edge
of the road, arms folded,
eyes unfocussed, expecting nothing

but more of the same. Dogs bark
staccato over the pulse of generators.
Washing flickers between the vans,
random semaphore, and clocks

run slow. Sun rises over the wasteland,
sets behind the chain link fence.
And on Sunday old Aunt Helen died.
Inside her trailer mourners fidget,

watched by the gold-haloed faces
of her best Crown Derby plates.
No-one speaks but half-words form
in the gas fire's popping, in the wind

around the broken door. Holding flowers
and a card he cannot read, brush-headed
Johnny, the boxer hero, racks tears
into a cushion. Sister Lizzie

glances sideways, gnaws a fingernail.
Traffic raises curtains in the rain
and Georgie stands where his mother
used to sit at night with her roll-ups

and her pint of tea. Arms folded
and his eyes unfocussed, he dreams
awake, pondering atavistic visions
of the fires of Little Egypt,

of the briar and the gorse,
of slower tides than these
that pull us all from history
and into the new lands.

NAMES OF THE MOON

Sucked pebble:
tongued smooth by black sand.
Starflecks on a sable field,
sour white, bleached as night,
juice dried, a flat splash.

Old coin:
dun metal edged like a
flint shard, spent, effaced,
the ghost profile watching
west, the setting point.

Bleached horns:
hook hanging, depending nothing
but planet-wrack,
clipped strings of light,
the dead hair of comets.

Broken button:
tugged and twined, frayed against
the cape and cowl, shrugged high
and loose in ice-heart
marrowbone dark.

Flat cataract:
milk or smoke or silica,
obscuring the macula, watching
only what she remembers
of red shift, of spectrum drift.

Abalone pearl:
infected by a flushed horizon
thus pink and purple,
elliptical meniscus,
frozen albumen.

Eyes in the night:
tsuki, menes,
chand, spogmay,
he'ni, loar,
namwaikaina.

SEEDS

We bought black seeds.
The plastic bag they came in
featured flowers – extravagant,
optimistic, like a prisoner's dream.

We tipped the seeds
into our palms. They rolled
like fairy bombs, fuseless
but ticking with promise.

We planted the seeds amongst
stones and watched the frantic
rain scouring the earth,
the sun, promiscuous, probing

the deep chambers. The birds
returned; the days passed then
stretched, like sleepers waking,
lifting dawns and dusks away.

And the flowers arrived
in a tumble, breathless and
coquettish. In love, we knelt
beside them, lifted their lolling

heads, importunate, outrageous, all
lips and tongues and hair
in tangles. And they teetered,
adoring themselves in an

undeserving world, while down
below the earthline dark and secret
feet gripped tight the shards
of black ancestor seeds.

MICHAEL COLLINS ORBITS THE MOON

I am elected watchman. It's my lot
to turn and turn in my tiny cradle. Not
to be my fortune or my obligation
to first-foot the moon and talk to nations.

Not for me grey beach or empty ocean,
nor earthlight or the silent locomotion
of the stars. Uncrowded by the legion voices
of the world I turn. The world rejoices

and I curl into the secret night
behind the moon. In amniotic light
I float, an embryo, a silver plan.
This egg will carry me unborn while man

takes giant steps below. And thus, unhatched,
Columbia's adrift, initials scratched
on incomprehensible darkness. I'm serene
in my awful solitude at sea between

the impassive weight of galaxies and the husk
of the moon. I close my eyes; a kind of dusk
prevails, half-memory of quotidian time,
a rhythm bound into the steady rhyme

of seasons. And I dream of the shifting grass
of prairies, mesas, lost highways that pass,
relentless and unbending, by outposts,
forts and cowtowns whose brave boothill ghosts

still ride the range. I dream of empty homesteads
whose screendoors bang on windy nights, tin sheds,
barbed wire and oil-well donkeys, one blind end
to the sand, the other to the stars. Old trails bend

and turn upon themselves where pioneers pause
inside their journeys to write down their laws
and call these scratches in the sand Jerusalem.
But night brings stars - still over Bethlehem

or here like a choir triumphant. As I ride
Columbia round the horn of moon, a tide
of voices wakes me, calling out the charter
of my race: small steps are mighty steps, *ad inexplorata*.

Acknowledgments

The author gratefully acknowledges the publications in which the following poems first appeared:

"Petal in a Book" — *Obsessed with Pipework* #48

"Birds by the Chusavaya" —*Westwords* #12

"The Sun Hotel, 1954" — *Foolscap* #15

"Michael Collins Orbits the Moon" — *Orbis* 80/81

"Sheep on the Brown Hill" — *Poetry Ireland Review* #61

"Shooting at a Fox" — *The Interpreter's House* #10

"The Ties that Bind" — *Brittle Star* #23

"Die Mauer ist Runte" — *Sing Freedom!* (Amnesty Anthology)

"Mal" — *Envoi* 127

"Between Stations," "Lines," "Night Rain," and "Still Life" — *qarrtsiluni*

So much is owed to the following for their support and assistance in bringing so many of these poems from the dark into the light via my blog, *Dick Jones' Patteran Pages*: Natalie d'Arbeloff, Lucy Kempton, Dominic Rivron, Beth Westmark, Dale Favier, Sam Mills, Dave King, John Hayes, Amy Barlow, Rachel Fenton, Jean Morris, Kass Feigal, Beth Adams, HKatz, Hannah Stephenson, Jim Murdoch, Rachel Rawlins, Dave Bonta, Tess Kincaid, Ailie Collins, Pat Thistlethwaite, Pauline Clarke.

Notes

pg 1. STILLE NACHT: I wrote this poem in the late '80s and it's always had particular significance for me, initiating as it did a series of autobiographical poems dealing with earliest memory.

I have no recollection of the War; I was only 9 months old when it ended. But its penumbra lay across the late '40s of my earliest recollection & into the 1950s of my childhood. The untouched bombsites of South London, acres of blank dereliction; the terraces of houses, their severed shored-up ends carrying the tracery of fireplaces, the ghost outlines of staircases; the air raid siren on its derrick by the tram station half way along Balham High Street. And most of all my parents' anecdotes: Mum, pregnant with me, blown along the corridor in our upstairs flat when a V2 destroyed the pub at the end of Emmanuel Road; my parents sitting in deckchairs on the flat roof of the block of flats where our friends the Kemps lived, watching the searchlights switching back & forth across the night sky during the bombing of the docklands; Dad in his Home Guard uniform, throwing hand grenades at concrete blocks on Wandsworth Common...

For all of us growing up at that time, the War provided the context wherein all assessment of present experience & future speculation was made. Even now I feel its immanence.

pg 21. ROS RUA: 'Ros Rua' is on the Galway coast, Eire.

pg 27. GRASSCUTTERS IN SVERDLOVSK: Sverdlovsk is in the Urals, near the border between Europe and Asia. It has reverted to its original name of Ekaterinburg.

pg 57. WAVELENGTHS. Glossary:

Icom 756 Pro Mk II HF transceiver - A ham radio transceiver, enabling the user to call and receive person-to-person radio transmissions on the wavebands allocated to licensed amateur radio operators.

05.00 zulu - A radio term for the Co-ordinated Universal Time zone (UTC).

Antenna tower/beaming west - The operator is using a horizontally-mounted aerial which he can turn to face in any compass direction, the better to transmit or receive radio signals.

20 meters - The busiest of the high frequency radio frequencies, operating on 14 mHz.

Heterodyne - A somewhat inexact application of a term meaning deliberate frequency combination but referring here to the characteristic oscillation of audio tones between specific frequencies.

The long path - A strategy whereby the aerial is turned 180 degrees away from Australia so as to send and receive signals across empty ocean rather than radio-busy land.

VK3 - An Australian callsign prefix registered in Victoria.

Skywave - Radio waves are refracted through the ionosphere whose density and composition shifts constantly. A signal may be lost suddenly or may fade away as the ionospheric clouds through which it is passing decompose.

pg 71. SIMON WIESENTHAL: Simon Wiesenthal, an Austrian Jew, was liberated from Mauthausen concentration camp by American troops on May 5th 1945. He went on to found the Simon Wiesenthal Centre, the Nazi-hunting organisation that, amongst many others, played a part in locating Adolf Eichmann.

pg 89. BEBEE HELEN'S MERRIPEN: *Bebee* means "aunt" and *merripen* means "death" in Anglo-Romani, the anglicised version of Romani, the language of the Roma people. 'Little Egypt' is a local place name that has emerged in several parts of the British Isles in which Gypsies have traditionally stopped (the erroneous belief being that Gypsies came originally from Egypt).

pg 94. MICHAEL COLLINS ORBITS THE MOON: While Neil Armstrong and Buzz Aldrin walked on the moon, Michael Collins piloted the lunar module as it passed around the far side.

About the Author

Initially wooed by the First World War poets and then seduced by the Beats, Dick Jones has been exploring the vast territories in between since the age of 15.

Dick's work has been published in a number of magazines, print and online, including *Orbis, The Interpreter's House, Poetry Ireland Review, Qarrtsiluni, Westwords, Mipoesias, Three Candles, Other Poetry, Rattlesnake* and *Ouroboros Review*, and in several print anthologies, including *Sing Freedom!* (Amnesty International), *Brilliant Coroners* (Phoenicia Publishing), and *Words of Power* (qarrtsiluni/Phoenicia). His chapbook, *Wavelengths*, was a finalist in the 2009 *qarrtsiluni* chapbook contest, and he was nominated for the Pushcart Prize in 2010 for his poem, "Sea of Stars."

In addition to thirty-five years of teaching drama in progressive schools, Dick Jones has been an avid musician all his life, playing bass guitar in rock, blues, and folk bands. He lives outside London with his wife and children, and blogs at *Dick Jones' Patteran Pages*, www.patteran.typepad.com

About the Cover

The cover illustration is by Rosemarie O'Toole, and is a handmade porcelain tile from Roundstone Ceramics, Connemara, Co. Galway, Ireland. roundstonepottery@eircom.net 003539535874

About Phoenicia Publishing

Phoenicia Publishing is a small independent press based in Montreal but involved, through a network of online connections, with writers and artists all over the world. We are interested in words and images that illuminate culture, spirit, and the human experience. A particular focus is on writing and art about travel between cultures—whether literally, through lives of refugees, immigrants, and travelers, or more metaphorically and philosophically—with the goal of enlarging our understanding of one another through universal and particular experiences of change, displacement, disconnection, assimilation, sorrow, gratitude, longing and hope.

We are committed to the innovative use of the web and digital technology in all aspects of publishing and distribution, and to making high-quality works available that might not be viable for larger publishers. We work closely with our authors, and are pleased to be able to offer them a greater share of royalties than is normally possible.

Your support of this endeavor is greatly appreciated.

Our complete catalogue is online at www.phoeniciapublishing.com

Made in the USA
Lexington, KY
30 April 2012